READING, WRITING, & MATH

GIFTED & TALENTED

Grade 4

Published by Frank Schaffer Publications
an imprint of

 Children's Publishing

Author: Vicky Shiotsu, Tracy Masonis
Editor: Melissa Warner Hale

 **Children's Publishing**

Published by Frank Schaffer Publications
An imprint of McGraw-Hill Children's Publishing
Copyright © 2003 McGraw-Hill Children's Publishing

Send all inquiries to:
McGraw-Hill Children's Publishing
3195 Wilson Drive NW
Grand Rapids, MI 49544

Gifted & Talented Reading, Writing, and Math – grade 4
ISBN 0-7682-2784-4

1 2 3 4 5 6 7 8 9 10 PHXBK 09 08 07 06 05 04

Table of Contents

Reading

Writing

Math

Circle a Synonym!

Words that mean the **same** thing, or nearly the same thing, are called **synonyms**. Circle a synonym for the **underlined** word in each row below. Then write another synonym from the Word List in the blanks.

Word List

rich	processed	same
easy	daring	assist

1. <u>prosperous</u>   mansion   wealthy   _____

2. <u>simple</u>   plain   plan   _____

3. <u>artificial</u>   flavor   fake   _____

4. <u>bold</u>   brave   warrior   _____

5. <u>uniform</u>   soldier   attire   _____

6. <u>support</u>   help   bridge   _____

Synonym Stars!

The synonym awards are here, and you are the director for the show! You need to make a great speech filled with the best synonyms possible. Change each underlined word in the speech below to a more exciting synonym. You may use the Word List for ideas.

Word List

trembling	elegant	moving	smart
rattling	celebration	enjoyable	giddy
approve of	lovely	extravaganza	effort
anxious	jittering	entertainment	
quiet	tense	respect	

Welcome to Synonym Stars! My hands are <u>shaking</u> with excitement for tonight's <u>performance</u>. Even though I am <u>nervous</u>, I am very happy to be here. The celebrities look <u>nice</u>, and the show will be <u>fun</u>. I hope you <u>like</u> our <u>work</u>, so sit back, relax, and enjoy!

Now write the new speech on the lines below.

_____

_____

_____

_____

_____

Name _____   Date _____

 Antonyms Are Opposites!

Words with **opposite** meanings are called **antonyms**. Circle the pair of antonyms in each box. Then complete each sentence with one of the circled words.

1. | stupid   average   boring   intelligent |

The judge said my ideas were very
_____ and that I was a winner!

Forgetting my lunch at home was a _____ mistake.

2. | confident   unkind   mysterious   unsure |

Because the soldier was prepared for battle,
he felt _____.

I felt _____ about how I would
perform because I did not practice much.

3. | defend   brave   courageous   attack |

I always try to _____
my friends when somebody teases them.

The defense prepared for the offense's _____.

4. | energetic   shiver   bold   lazy |

Eating nutritious food helps people feel _____.

Not getting the proper amount of exercise
will make you feel _____.

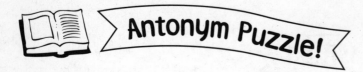

Antonym Puzzle!

Can you fill in the crossword puzzle below?
Use the words in the Word List as clues.
Choose each word's **opposite** meaning
and write that word in the puzzle. Good luck!

Word List

Across	Down
1. expensive	2. graceful
4. often	3. less
6. fiction	4. antonym
7. polite	5. fierce

Different Meanings

Some words have more than one meaning. Look at the words below and read each of their multiple meanings. Now look at the pictures. Next to each picture write the number of the meaning that correctly identifies it.

train: **1.** a connected line of railroad cars
         2. to prepare physically

light: **3.** not dark, bright
         4. to set fire to something
         5. graceful, moving quickly and easily

left: **6.** went away
         7. the opposite of right

_____   _____   _____

 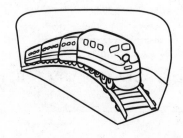  

_____   _____   _____   _____

0-7682-2784-4 *Gifted & Talented Reading, Writing, and Math*

Name _____ Date _____

 Check, Please!

Some words have more than one meaning. Look at the list below. Two different meanings are given for each word.

Ⓐ   Ⓑ

bill: notice of money owed   a bird's beak

check: to check something   a means of paying for
            off a list   something

stock: domestic animals kept   a piece of ownership
            on a farm   in a company

trade: an exchange of one   an occupation or job
            thing for another

deposit: sum of money   minerals or sandy matter
            placed in a bank   placed by moving water

Now choose which meaning from the list matches the **boldfaced** word in each sentence below. Fill in the A or B circle accordingly. Then write the meaning you chose on the line.

1. ⒶⒷ Plumbing is my **trade**. _____

2. ⒶⒷ I just got paid, so I need to make a **deposit** at the bank.

   _____

3. ⒶⒷ **Check** that off the list, please. _____

4. ⒶⒷ I hope to buy **stock** in the ABC Company someday.

   _____

5. ⒶⒷ Do you have enough money to pay your phone **bill**?

   _____

Name _____   Date _____

Common Corrections!

Some words look and sound very much alike but have very different meanings. Look at the words and meanings below. Then write the correct word to complete each sentence.

their: pronoun used to indicate possession or ownership

there: at or in that place

angel: a figure with halo and wings

angle: figure made by two lines coming from a single point

accept: to answer affirmatively; to say *yes*

except: with the exclusion of; otherwise

intend: to have in mind; plan

attend: to be present at

1. I want to visit _____ house.

2. I _____ your invitation to go _____.

3. I think _____ house is beautiful _____ for the olive-green kitchen wallpaper.

4. The photographer took pictures of two _____ (s) with his wide _____ camera.

5. I _____ to _____ _____ party.

More Common Corrections!

Some words look and sound very much alike but have very different meanings. Fill in the sentences below using the correct words from the Word List.

Word List

series	lose	bear
serious	loose	bare

1. I love collecting an entire _____ of comic books.

2. The power button on my television is _____ .

3. The tree will _____ luscious fruit.

4. We need to have a _____ talk.

5. I will never _____ this journal.

6. The _____ wall really needs some pictures.
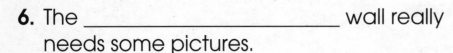

>Claudio's Context Clues!<

When you read, it's important to look for context clues. **Context clues** can help you figure out the meaning of a word, or a missing word, just by looking at the **other words** in the sentence.

Read each sentence below. Circle the context clues or other words in the sentence that give you hints. Then choose a word from the Word List to replace the **boldfaced** word. Write it on the line.

Word List		
walking	announced	fun
grow	sprinting	touch

1. Watering my flowers will help them **flourish**.

   _____

2. When I gently **caress** my baby brother's cheek, he smiles. _____

3. I like **sauntering** through the park and watching all the birds. _____

4. I had a **jovial** time at the outrageous party!

   _____

5. The judge **proclaimed** me the winner of the boysenberry pie-eating contest.

   _____

What Do You Mean?

Choose a word from the Word List to replace the **boldfaced** word in each sentence. Write the word on the line. Use a dictionary to help you with any new words.

Word List

fat	awful	strutting
shouting	skinny	empty

1. The **obese** elephant must have weighed 10 tons! _____

2. The **clamor** from the lion's den frightened me. _____

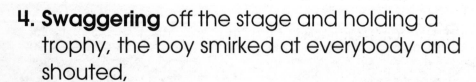

3. The skunk emitted a **repugnant** odor when a predator drew near him.
_____

4. **Swaggering** off the stage and holding a trophy, the boy smirked at everybody and shouted,
"I am the best!" _____

5. The island remained **desolate** for 100 years.
_____

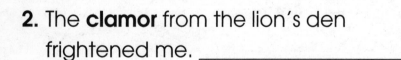

Name _____   Date _____

Mind the Mold!

Choose the best meaning for the **underlined** word in the sentences below. Circle your choice.

"Pour the hot wax into the candle <u>mold</u>," said Ms. Galloway, my art teacher. "We will let it cool for a few hours and then remove the new candle."

1. the outer layer of the earth

2. a fuzzy growth

3. a form for making something into a certain shape

"Remember to <u>mind</u> your grandma," said my mom, as she dropped me off at Grandma's house.

1. bump heads with someone

2. to follow someone's directions

3. think about

The restaurant served its bread with a little <u>pat</u> of butter on the side of each plate.

1. a small, individual portion

2. to gently tap someone's head or hand

3. a small dog

Figure It Out!

An **idiom** is a figure of speech. An **idiom phrase** means something different than what it actually says. After each sentence, draw an **X** in front of the meaning that best describes the underlined idiom phrase.

I. When the principal's toupee flew off his head, Melanie sat at her desk and tried to <u>keep a straight face</u>.

_____Melanie tried to remain serious.

_____Melanie tried to laugh.

_____Melanie tried to have fun.

2. Joey is trying to make the academic honor roll. In order to accomplish this, Joey needs to <u>keep his nose to the grindstone</u>.

_____Joey plans to study every night.

_____Joey plans to study a few nights each week.

_____Joey plans to study for a few minutes each night and then play basketball.

3. Alexis and Molly have a new gerbil. One night, the gerbil escaped and zoomed all around the house. The girls chased the gerbil everywhere, but they became exhausted. That gerbil <u>ran them ragged</u>.

_____The gerbil ripped the girls' clothes into rags.

_____The gerbil made the girls very tired.

_____The gerbil made the girls angry.

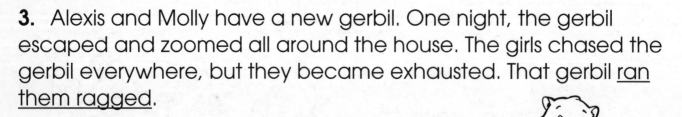

Figure It Out!

4. A storm swept through the area. The weather forecaster said, "It will be <u>raining cats and dogs</u> tonight, so be careful."

_____ The rain would be severe and heavy.

_____ The rain would be a steady drizzle.

_____ The rain would not bother anybody.

5. Liza has a lovely garden, ripe with all sorts of healthy plants. In fact, it seems like everything she plants grows. She is said to have <u>a green thumb</u>.

_____ Liza's thumb is green in color.

_____ Liza is a successful gardener.

_____ Liza wraps a green leaf around her thumb.

6. Lenka came home from school and started crying profusely. Her mother asked her what happened. Lenka told her mother that she lost her lunch card after school. Her mother said, "Lenka, <u>do not cry over spilled milk</u>. You will get a new one tomorrow."

_____ Do not worry about the small things.

_____ Do not lose anything again.

_____ It is not your fault.

0-7682-2784-4 *Gifted & Talented Reading, Writing, and Math*

The Recycler

Hi there!

A **character** is the person, animal, or object that a story is about. You cannot have a story without a character.

Characters are usually people, but sometimes they can be animals, aliens (!), or even objects that come to life. You can have many characters in a story.

Read the story below. Then answer the questions about character on the next page.

Sasha is president of the Recycling Club at her school. She meets with the 40 members in the club every week. At the meetings, she says, "We need to brainstorm ways to protect our environment! We need to stop adding unnecessary waste to landfills!"

Sasha came up with the idea of placing blue recycling bins next to every wastebasket in the school to recycle soda cans. She also put a recycling bin next to the teachers' copy machine that says, "Please, recycle." Sasha is very passionate about recycling.

At home, she organized and labeled her family's three trash cans. One is for paper waste, one is for aluminum cans and glass, and one is for regular waste. Her parents call her "The Recycler!" Sasha knows how important it is to protect the Earth, and recycling is a big part of doing that.

More About the Recycler!

First, authors must decide who the main character is going to be in their story. Then they reveal the character's personality by:

what the character does
what the character says
what other people say about the character

Give two examples of what Sasha **does** to show that she is passionate about recycling.

1. _____

2. _____

Give an example of what Sasha **says** to reveal that she is passionate about recycling.

_____

Give an example of what **other people say** about Sasha and her recycling efforts.

_____

If Sasha drank a soda at a park and there was no recycling bin for the can, what do you think she would do? What would you do? Write your answers on the lines below.

_____

_____

Amundsen-Scott Station

Read the story below and then answer the questions about the setting.

There is a place on Earth that is very cold and very icy. The few planes that travel there must have skis attached to their undersides so that they can land! This place is the continent of Antarctica, the coldest place on Earth. In fact, the coldest temperature on the entire planet was recorded in Antarctica in July of 1983. It was more than 100 degrees below zero! Actually, it was –128.6° Fahrenheit, to be exact.

Ninety percent of the world's ice is in Antarctica. It is a continent over 5,000,000 square miles in area and is owned by no country. A small number of scientific research stations set up by a few countries that have claimed territory in Antarctica fill the continent. The Amundsen-Scott station is an American scientific research station in Antarctica named after Roald Amundsen and Robert Scott. Amundsen was the first person to ever reach the South Pole. He did so in December of 1911. Scott, from the United Kingdom, reached the South Pole a month later in January of 1912.

Amundsen-Scott Station

Scientists who stay at the station today have to be very careful because of the dangerous climate. There are only six months of sunlight and then six months of darkness. In the summer months, the scientists must be careful to protect their eyes from the constant sunlight reflecting off the snow and ice. All of that sunlight can actually burn their eyes and cause blindness. At times, the wind can be fierce, and it howls over the ice. This makes it even colder and more difficult to see.

Antarctica has one of the harshest climates on Earth. Even so, many scientists who visit it say that all of the pure, white ice makes it one of the most beautiful places on Earth.

What would you **see** if you visited the Amundsen-Scott station in Antarctica? _____

_____

_____

What might you **hear** living at the station? _____

_____

_____

What would you **feel** living at the station? _____

_____

_____

Happy Kwanzaa!

The **setting** is the **place** where the story happens. The setting is also the **time** in which the story takes place. A reader needs to know **when** the story is happening. Does it take place at night? On a sunny day? In the future? During the winter?

Time can be: time of day
   a holiday
     a season of the year
     a time in history
     a time in the future

Read the following story. Then answer the questions below.

Kwanzaa is the name of an African-American holiday. It is named after the Swahili phrase, "Matunda ya kwanzaa," which means "first fruits." This holiday starts on December 26 and lasts through January 1. It commemorates African tribes coming together to sing, eat, dance, and celebrate the bounty of their fruit and vegetable harvests. Aisha celebrates Kwanzaa with her family. On December 31, there is a big feast. All of Aisha's relatives come over in the evening to share food, gifts, and song. If you ever celebrate Kwanzaa, make sure you can say, "Kwanzaa Yenu iwe na heri," which means, of course, "Happy Kwanzaa!"

1. When does the holiday of Kwanzaa take place?

_____

2. At what time and on what day do Aisha's relatives come over to celebrate the Kwanzaa feast?

_____

Name _____   Date _____

When and Where?

The **setting** tells **when** and **where** a story takes place. Read the story settings below. Then describe where and when each story takes place.

The balmy night air of San Juan feels nice against my skin. I often visit my Aunt Sylvia, who lives in San Juan, the capital of Puerto Rico. She says Puerto Rico has the best weather in the world. Other people say that during the winter months, only in Puerto Rico can you feel such warm, soft air.

1. When did this story take place? _____

2. Where did this story take place? _____

Last June, Regan traveled to an exotic destination. After working hard all year, she wanted to swim, read books, and relax. She found the vacation spot she was looking for when she visited the beautiful beaches of Costa Rica!

3. When did this story take place? _____

4. Where did this story take place? _____

The snowflakes fell hard on my face. My mittens were covered with snow. Even so, there was no way I was going to leave the November Championship Game at Rigby Field! I came here to root for my favorite team!

5. When did this story take place? _____

6. Where did this story take place? _____

0-7682-2784-4 *Gifted & Talented Reading, Writing, and Math*

Name _____   Date _____

Make a Map!

Think about a story or book you have read. Did the character take a journey or walk around his or her town? In your imagination, what does your character's home look like? Where did the main events in the story take place? Keeping your story in mind and following the directions below, create a detailed map showing the place where the characters lived.

1. Draw the outline of your map on a sheet of paper.

2. Be sure to write the title and the author of the book at the top of the map.

3. Think about what places you want to include on your map, and then draw them.

4. Label the important places, adding a brief phrase or sentence about what happened there.

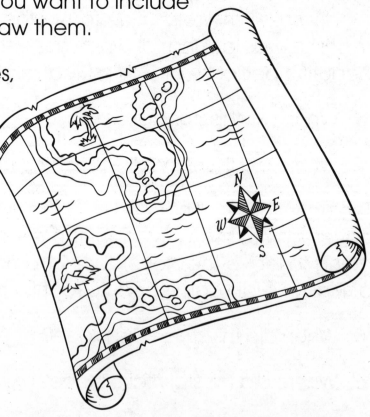

5. Add color and details.

6. Share your map with friends and tell them about the story you read.

0-7682-2784-4 *Gifted & Talented Reading, Writing, and Math*

Gee Whiz, Genres!

Some stories are true and some are imaginary. **Fiction** stories are not real. They are made up. **Nonfiction** stories are true. All of the stories below are fiction. However, the three stories are from different genres. A **genre** is a category or type of literature. Some examples of different genres are listed below.

An **autobiography** is the story of a person's life written by that person.

A **biography** is a book written about the life of a person by another person.

An **informational passage** gives information about a subject.

Read the passages on the following pages. Then write what genre they would be classified as: **biography**, **autobiography**, or **informational passage**.

Suzette La Fleur!

The planet De Fleur is a space colony located between Earth and Mars. Its only purpose is to grow flowers. Suzette La Fleur founded the planet. This great lady is now the queen of planet De Fleur. In the beginning, 50 people and 1,000,000 different flower seeds were brought by space shuttle to the planet. It soon became the largest greenhouse in the universe. The greenhouse now covers an entire planet and is the best international space florist. All flower deliveries in outer space come from the planet De Fleur.

1. What genre is this? _____

Hello, my name is Suzette La Fleur, and I am the queen of the planet De Fleur. People always ask me about my life and the challenges I face being the queen of De Fleur. I always tell them about a time when I turned adversity into triumph. I was very frustrated. Pesky comets kept zooming by my greenhouse, changing the light rays that beam at my flowers. I worked with my team of scientists to develop some high-powered zappers. Now, if erratic comets or other space debris heads towards my flowers, they are zapped and turned into fertilizer. I love living on planet De Fleur and being the best florist in the universe!

2. What genre is this? _____

Suzette La Fleur!

Suzette La Fleur is an amazing entrepreneur. She was born on the planet Earth in a small farming town in Iowa. It was there that she first fell in love with flowers. Twenty years later, when there was an intergalactic need for flowers, Suzette La Fleur took a bold move that no human had ever thought of before. She created an intergalactic space greenhouse that uses the sun's rays to grow flowers!

Suzette's elementary school classmates said that even as a young child, Suzette was always creative, thinking up new solutions to problems. Suzette was proclaimed the queen of the planet De Fleur in the year 2088.

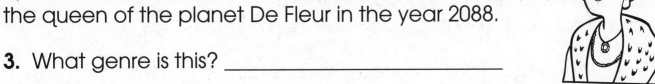

3. What genre is this? _____

4. Now pick a genre—autobiography, biography, or informational passage—and write a story in this genre on the lines below.

_____

_____

_____

_____

_____

_____

_____

Name _____   Date _____

How Do Giraffes Drink?

Read the story below. As you read it, look for clues that tell you the order in which things happened. Then answer the questions about the sequence of events on the next page.

Giraffes are gentle giants! They are very tall and very gentle. They live in small herds and like to eat twigs and leaves. Their super long legs help them run very fast, up to 47 miles per hour. Their legs also help them to stand tall and see at a great distance.

Their long legs make it quite awkward for them to drink though! When a giraffe wants to take a drink, it must first find water. Then it has to plant its back two legs firmly and spread its front two legs very wide. Its front legs are longer than its back legs, which adds to its drinking difficulty!

Next, the giraffe must lower its neck between its front legs and suck in water. The giraffe's neck is so long that it must use its throat to suck the water up its long neck into its stomach! Maybe somebody should invent an extra long giraffe straw to make drinking easier for it!

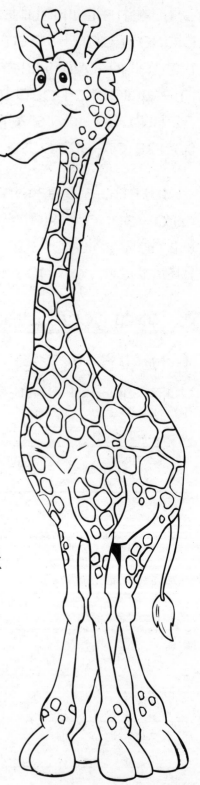

0-7682-2784-4 *Gifted & Talented Reading, Writing, and Math*

Okay, So How Do They Do It?

Below are the steps a giraffe must take in order to get a drink of water, but they are all mixed up! Number the steps in order. Draw an **X** in front of any step that is not needed.

_____ Use throat to suck water up long neck to stomach.

_____ Find watering hole.

_____ Spread front two legs very wide.

_____ Round up herd of giraffes.

_____ Eat twigs and leaves.

_____ Pose for tourists' pictures.

_____ Suck in water.

_____ Plant back legs firmly for balance.

_____ Spit water at another giraffe for laughing at strange leg position.

_____ Gently eat leaves high up in tree.

_____ Lower neck between front legs.

_____ Buy straws.

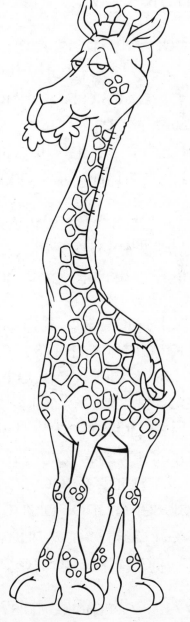

0-7682-2784-4 *Gifted & Talented Reading, Writing, and Math*

Name _____   Date _____

Dirt Cake!

Read the story on the following pages. As you read it, look for clues that tell you the order in which things happened.

"First, we need a snack," said Tiffany, as the front door of her house closed behind us. I followed Tiffany down a long corridor and into her kitchen. This is the first time Tiffany had invited me over to her house to play.

"Oh look, my mom left us a note," said Tiffany. The kitchen table was covered in a pretty tablecloth and on it was a flower in a pot. In front of it was a note that read, "Here is a fun snack for you and Erica. Love, Mom." Tiffany smiled. "Oh, wow. I love it when my mom makes this!" she said. Tiffany got out two spoons and took a big bite of the soil from the flowerpot!

"Tiffany! Oh, my gosh! What are you doing?! You are eating plant dirt!" I screamed, horrified. Tiffany smiled and took another big spoonful. Brown dirt covered her face.

"No, I am not, silly. It is crushed Oreos, not dirt, and this is my mom's special 'Dirt Cake,' not a plant! Here, you try some," said Tiffany smiling. She gave me the spoon, and I dug into the "dirt." It tasted like pudding and Oreo cookies. I looked closer at the "plant." Tiffany's mom even put some gummy worms in the dirt for us to eat!

"How do you make this?" I asked.

0-7682-2784-4 *Gifted & Talented Reading, Writing, and Math*

 Dirt Cake!

"Easy," said Tiffany. "First, line a flowerpot with aluminum foil. Then mix together in a bowl, 1 large container of instant whipped cream, 1 instant pudding mix, and 1 jar of cherries. Then, put the whole mix in the lined flowerpot. Next, take 15–20 Oreos and crush them in a paper bag. Sprinkle the Oreo "dirt" on ___ of the flowerpot. Add a few gummy worms to the surface "s___ ___ fake flower in the center of the flowerpot. There ___ ___ Cake—my favorite after-school snack!" sa___

Now answer the questions a___ ___ ___swers.

1. What happened first?

   A. Erica follows Tiffany ___ ___ ___ ___ ___ ___tchen.

   B. Erica is invited ove___

   C. Erica forgets her sn___ ___ ___me.

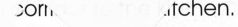

2. After Tiffany finds the note from her mom, what happens?

   A. Tiffany finds a worm in the dirt.

   B. Tiffany gets out two spoons.

   C. Tiffany reads the note.

3. When did Erica eat some of the Dirt Cake?

   A. After Tiffany tells her what is in it.

   B. After Tiffany gives her a spoon.

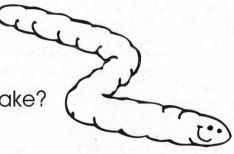

   C. After Tiffany tells her how to make it.

Dirt Cake!

4. What is the first step in making Dirt Cake?

    A. Mix whipped cream, pudding, and cherries in a bowl.

    B. Line a flowerpot with aluminum foil.

    C. Buy ingredients at the store.

5. What is the first step in making soil for Dirt Cake?

    A. Place the Oreos on the top layer of the flowerpot.

    B. Put the Oreos into a paper bag.

    C. Crush the Oreos finely and sprinkle them onto the top layer of the cake.

6. What could you add to make Dirt Cake even more exciting?

    A. Worms

    B. Gummy worms

    C. Candy frogs

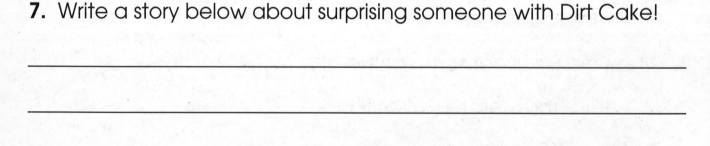

7. Write a story below about surprising someone with Dirt Cake!

_____

_____

_____

_____

Mindy Gets the Main Idea!

The **main idea** is what a story is about. Help Mindy figure out the main idea of the passages below. Write a check mark next to each main idea.

Sammy spends much of his free time at homeless shelters and soup kitchens. He also gives time to many local charities.

1. What is the main idea?

_____ Sammy is a hard worker.

_____ Sammy is busy.   _____ Sammy is unselfish.

Jamie developed a business plan. He decided to make inexpensive sunglasses that don't break. Jamie made the glasses and sold them. In addition, he created the advertisements for his product. His company became an overnight success.

2. What is the main idea?

_____ Jamie must be tired.   _____ Jamie is a popular person.

_____ Jamie is an intelligent businessman.

Mr. Waterford loves the taste of fast food! He enjoys the smell of the greasy grill, and he certainly loves sinking his teeth into a tasty cheeseburger.

3. What is the main idea?

_____ Mr. Waterford must have high cholesterol.

_____ Mr. Waterford enjoys visiting fast-food places.

_____ Mr. Waterford loves French fries.

Flying Penguins

Read the story below. Then circle the letter choice of the sentence that tells the main idea of the story.

There are 17 different types of penguins. Penguins are birds that cannot fly. They all have wings, but none of them can use them to fly! Their wings are used as flippers, which help them "fly" through the water. Their bodies are specially streamlined like torpedoes. This enables them to shoot out of the water and onto the ice or rocks in one leap!

Most birds have light, hollow bones that minimize their weight and help them to fly. Penguins have solid bones, which adds weight and helps them dive deep under water.

Swimming fast and diving deep are critical abilities that penguins need so that they can escape from predators, such as killer whales or leopard seals. Penguins are very special birds.

What is the main idea?

A. There are 17 different types of penguins.

B. Penguins cannot fly.

C. Penguins are designed with special features to help them survive.

 ╟ **Highlight Happy!**

Highlighting is a strategy that will help you with your reading. When you highlight something, use a light-colored marker to color over a special word or words that you want to remember.

Follow the directions to highlight the important words in the sentences below.

1. Highlight the capitals of three states.

   Many people know the names of all fifty states, but very few people can name all fifty state capitals. Some of the hardest state capitals to remember are Columbus, Ohio, and Columbia, South Carolina. People often get these two state capitals confused. Bismarck, North Dakota, and Pierre, South Dakota, are often mixed up as well. Also, many people think Chicago is the capital of Illinois, not Springfield.

2. Highlight two things you should remember.

   You should highlight words or phrases that will help you remember your thoughts.

Cause and Effect

Cause: An action or act that makes something happen.

Effect: Something that happens because of an action or cause.

Look at the following example of cause and effect.

Cause: We left our hot dogs on the grill too long.

Effect: Our hot dogs were burnt!

Read the story below. Then write the missing effect.

Walter went to the art gallery to see the Picasso exhibit. He examined many of the paintings and felt inspired to paint himself. He visited the library and read about Picasso. He found out that many of Picasso's paintings had been influenced by African art and masks. Walter was now extremely excited to learn more about Picasso's art.

Cause: Walter researched about African art.

Effect: _____

         0-7682-2784-4 *Gifted & Talented Reading, Writing, and Math*

Name _____   Date _____

How Did It Happen?

Read the stories below. Then write the missing cause or effect.

James traveled on a long plane ride. When he arrived at his destination, he had to change his watch back 6 hours. When his friend asked him to go to dinner at 6 p.m., James said, "I am sorry, but not now."

1. **Cause:** _____

   Effect: James could not make it to dinner.

Trudy's back ached because she had lifted heavy boxes all day long. Trudy set up an appointment at the yoga studio to work on stretching her muscles. Trudy learned new techniques and practiced them every day.

2. **Cause:** _____

   Effect: Trudy learned yoga.

Name _____   Date _____

Who Invented the Ice-Cream Cone?

Read the story below. Then answer the questions.

"Dad, who invented the ice-cream cone?" asked Cody.

"What a good question! Lots of people claim to have invented the ice-cream cone, but the two most famous stories about how the ice-cream cone was invented include Italo Marchiony and Ernest Hamwi."

"Marchiony immigrated to New York City from Italy and sold ice cream from a cart. He wanted people to stop walking off with his cups that held the ice cream. So in 1896, he invented the ice-cream cone. In December 1903, he was granted a patent for it," he explained.

"What is a patent?" asked Cody.

"A patent helps protect your idea or invention if you don't want it to be copied. The other popular story about the invention of the ice-cream cone was in 1904 at the St. Louis World's Fair."

"The story says that there was an ice-cream booth at the fair, and the ice-cream vendor ran out of bowls to serve his ice cream. It was still early in the day. Desperately, he looked at the booth next to him and saw Ernest Hamwi selling a waffle-type pastry called a *Zalabia*. Mr. Hamwi said he had an idea

Who Invented the Ice-Cream Cone?

to solve the ice-cream vendor's problem. He then rolled one of his waffle Zalabias into a cone. The cone cooled, the ice-cream vendor filled it with ice cream. The rest is ice-cream history!"

Use the information from the story to fill in the missing cause or effect below.

Cause	Effect
People kept walking off with Italo's ice-cream bowls.	1. _____
Italo wanted to protect his ice-cream cone idea.	2. _____
3. _____	The ice-cream vendor was desperate.
The ice-cream vendor looked at the booth next to him.	4. _____
Mr. Hamwi rolled one of his waffle-like pastries into a cone and let it cool.	5. _____

Read the story on the following pages. Then answer the questions.

"Mom, can we get a puppy?" asked Parnel.

"Yes, Parnel, but only one from the pound," replied his mother.

"What is the pound?" asked Parnel.

"The pound is a place where lost, abandoned, or rescued animals are brought. Mostly the pound holds dogs and cats, but it has some rabbits, too. There are a lot of animals that desperately need a good home, so it is best to go there first before buying one from a store. Let's see if there is a puppy at the pound that needs a home."

First, Parnel's mom called the pound to see when the animal visiting hours were. People can visit the animals at only certain times of the day because the animals need to eat, exercise, and sleep.

Parnel and his mom arrived at the pound. There were rows and rows of cages holding different kinds of dogs. There were old dogs, fat dogs, skinny dogs, sweet sleeping puppies, and loud barking dogs. There was another row of cages holding orange-striped kittens, soft-purring cats, and meowing kittens who stuck their noses through the metal grates. There was even a row of cages holding all different types of rabbits.

Parnel stuck his hand close to the cage of an old, yellow Labrador retriever. The dog licked Parnel's hand. "Hey, that tickles!" said Parnel. The dog stuck out his old, soft tongue and licked Parnel again. Then Parnel saw a little white kitten curled up into a ball with her stomach rising up and down like a billowing tent. "She looks like a cotton ball!" said Parnel and stroked her soft tummy.

Parnel Picks Some Pets!

Parnel's mom was busy petting a spotted bunny with the biggest, floppiest ears she had ever seen. "Well, do you see a puppy you like, Parnel?" asked his mom.

"Actually, I was thinking the old Labrador looks like he needs a home the most, and the kitten sure looks cute!"

"Oh, Parnel, you are as bad as me! Let's ask the veterinarian if we can adopt the dog, the kitten, and the rabbit!"

Parnel hugged his mom, and they went to sign the adoption papers for their new pets.

Now answer the questions below.

Choose two words to describe Parnel's mom.

_____

Choose two words to describe Parnel. _____

Why are there so many animals in the pound? _____

_____

Why do you think Parnel chose to adopt the old Labrador retriever over a new puppy? _____

_____

What do you think will happen when Parnel and his mom get home with their three new pets? _____

_____

500 Apples!

Read the story below. Then answer the question at the bottom of the page.

One day, a rickety old pickup truck stopped outside of my house. It was full of hundreds of red apples. The driver of the truck waved and called out the window, "Good morning, folks! You are the lucky winners of 500 red apples! Where would you like them?"

Use your imagination and tell what you think happens next in the story.

_____

_____

_____

_____

_____

What Happens Next?

Read each paragraph below. Predict what will happen next in the story by placing an **X** in front of the best answer.

Jonathan met the old master chess player in the park for the sixth week in a row. Each week, the old master beat him at chess. Even still, Jonathan knew that he was getting better at chess. "Jonathan, you have a natural talent for playing chess. Every five years I take on one new pupil if I think he or she can handle my training."

_____ Jonathan gives up the game of chess.

_____ Jonathan accepts but soon finds he cannot handle the training.

_____ Jonathan accepts and one day beats the old master at a game.

_____ Jonathan says that he is content to just meet the master in the park.

Martha loves to bake cookies. Every day after school, she experiments with a new recipe. Oftentimes, she sells her most delicious recipes to stores and gives away samples to her friends.

_____ Martha will open her own cookie store one day.

_____ Martha will soon tire of baking cookies.

_____ Martha decides she wants to make more difficult desserts.

Naming Words—Nouns

A word that names a **person**, **place**, or **thing** is called a **noun**.

person

- chef
- postman
- florist

place

- meadow
- beach
- island

thing

- bowl
- dooknob
- jacket

Read the story below and circle all the nouns.

There is a magical chef who lives on a small, windy island off the coast of Ireland. His name is Happy O'Reilly, and people travel from all over the world to see Happy. He has jolly red cheeks, twinkling blue eyes, and a smile for everybody.

He lives by himself in a small, stone cottage that has a giant stone fireplace right in the middle. In that magical fireplace, he makes his potato bread and vegetable-beef stew that will cure any sickness. In the summertime, it is where he makes his apple cobbler dessert, which will keep a smile on your face for an entire year! Go visit Happy O'Reilly—if you can find him!

Name _____   Date _____

Action Words—Verbs

A word that tells what is happening in a sentence is called a **verb**. Write a verb in each blank. Use the word list to help you.

Word List			
answers	play	studies	race
read	eats	yell	hugs
dances	swims	chats	

Sara has a busy day at school. First, she _____ the teacher's question, and then she _____ for her spelling test. At 11:30 a.m., she _____ her lunch and _____ with her friends. On the playground at recess, the kids _____ each other and _____ at the top of their lungs! Sara likes to _____ quietly or _____ checkers instead!

Choose three of your favorite action words from the list above. Then write a sentence or more using all three words on the lines below.

_____

_____

Name _____ Date _____

Describing Words—Adjectives

A word that **describes** a noun is called an **adjective**. Fill in each blank below using the adjectives from the word lists.

Word List		
black	ugly	thousands
soft	expensive	hairy

1. The _____ mattress was very
   _____ to buy because it was
   made of _____ of downy feathers.

2. The _____, _____ spider
   was so _____ that everybody was afraid
   to look at him. All he really needed was a haircut!

Word List		
hungry	delicate	loud
beautiful	tall	scary

3. Brown bears can be very _____
   when they are _____. They stand up
   _____ and let out _____ growls.

4. Roses are _____ flowers and quite
   _____. Their petals feel like smooth velvet.

0-7682-2784-4 *Gifted & Talented Reading,
Writing, and Math*

Sentences—Complete Thoughts

A **sentence** tells a complete thought. It has a **subject**—what or who the sentence is about, and it has a **predicate**—what happened to the subject or what the subject did.

A **fragment** is **not a complete thought**.

Sentences: The museum was open.
               The movie starts at three o'clock.
               Mr. Tillbury is coming for dinner.

Fragments: Because Mr. Tillbury.
               The museum.
               Starts at three o'clock.

Write **sentence** on the line after each sentence. Write **fragment** on the line after each fragment.

1. Because I like chocolate.   _____
2. Paris is in France.   _____
3. Nina likes fritters.   _____
4. Washington, D.C., the capital   _____
   of the USA.
5. The ancient ruins of the Incas.   _____

Look at the four fragments below. Make them into sentences.

6. Likes to cook.   _____
7. Mr. Tillbury.   _____
8. Because fritters taste good.   _____
9. To bring to dinner.   _____

Name _____   Date _____

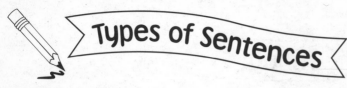
Types of Sentences

There are four main types of sentences: **declarative**, **interrogative**, **exclamatory**, and **imperative**.

A sentence that states something is called a **declarative** sentence. It ends with a period.

She wears a lovely dress.

He is tall.

A sentence that asks a question is called an **interrogative** sentence. It ends with a question mark.

How did you do that magic trick?

What is your name?

A sentence that shows strong emotion is called an **exclamatory** sentence. It always ends with an exclamation point.

Oh, no, fire!

Watch out!

A sentence that gives an order or command is called an **imperative** sentence. It ends with a period or an exclamation point.

Close the door.

Catch that before it falls!

0-7682-2784-4 *Gifted & Talented Reading, Writing, and Math*

The Commas Are Coming!

Use commas in an introductory clause:

Apart from his uncle Abner is the strangest in the family.

Talk about confusion!!

Is this even a sentence? Should "uncle" be capitalized?

Watch what a comma can do!

New sentence 1: Apart from his uncle, Abner is the strangest in the family.

New sentence 2: Apart from his Uncle Abner, <u>Jerome</u> is the strangest in the family!

If the underlined part were not added, a fragment would exist.

Now you try! Look at the examples below and add commas where they are necessary. Remember that a comma's main job is to clear up confusing sentences.

1. My three favorite foods are spinach ice cream and ham.

2. "Did you eat Jim?" Molly asked sincerely.

3. According to Billy Molly and Jim were up late last night trying to find apples cheese and desserts.

4. Looking back at her younger brother Molly stuck out her tongue!

5. After she left her aunt Susan started to cry.

Transition Words

In some paragraphs, the order or sequence of the sentences is very important. **Transition words**, such as **first, next, after, then, finally,** and **last**, offer clues to help show the sequence of the sentences.

Read the story below and circle the transition words.

    My brother is convinced that he makes the best apple pie in the world! He claims he has tried over 100 different recipes and has found the perfect one.

    First, he says it's all about the apples. He is convinced you must use only hand-picked Granny Smith apples. Next, you must carefully slice all the apples. After you have sliced them, you must add white and brown sugar, nutmeg, lemon juice, and butter. Then, you need to preheat the oven while you make the crust. Finally, when the crust is ready, you put the apples in the crust and bake at 350 degrees for a perfect apple pie!

Using Transition Words

In some paragraphs, the order or sequence of the sentences is very important.

Transition Words		
first	after	finally
next	then	last

The events below are in the correct order. Choose **transition words** from the box above to write these events in a complete paragraph. The topic sentence is written for you.

President Lincoln is considered one of the greatest presidents America has ever had. However, his road to greatness wasn't always easy. He failed many times, yet always persevered.

In 1854, Lincoln was defeated for the U. S. Senate.

In 1856, he experienced another defeat for the nomination of vice-president.

He again decided to run for the U.S. Senate even though he had lost once already in 1854.

He was defeated again for the United States Senate in 1858.

Abraham Lincoln was elected president in 1860, and steered the United States through a very difficult time.

Introducing the Five Senses

It is important to understand and to use your five senses so that you can fully enjoy the world and all the exciting things in it. The five senses are:

Sight—What you see

Sound—What you hear

Smell—What you smell

Taste—What you taste

Touch—What you feel

The next few exercises allow you to use your fantastic senses! Look at the pictures super carefully. Think about what things might look like, sound like, smell and taste like, and especially, what things might feel like. Have fun!

List three things you can see: _____

List three things you can hear: _____

List three things you can smell: _____

List three things you can taste: _____

List three things you can feel: _____

Name _____   Date _____

Look very carefully at the picture below. Study it closely. Then answer the questions on the next page.

Sense Exercise—Sight

Write your answers on the lines below.

1. What two foods are for sale at the intergalactic rest stop?

    _____

2. What are the Earth parents doing? _____

    _____

3. What do they fill their gas tanks with? _____

    _____

4. What are the two Earth children carrying? _____

    _____

5. What are the two space children carrying? _____

    _____

Sense Exercise—Sound

Look very carefully at the picture below. Study it closely. Then answer the questions on the next page.

0-7682-2784-4 *Gifted & Talented Reading, Writing, and Math*

Sense Exercise—Sound

What sound is the hammer-shaped doorbell making?

_____

What sounds are the cat and dog doorbells making?

_____

What does the cloud doorbell sound like?

_____

What does the rooster doorbell sound like when
   it is pushed?

_____

What does the regular doorbell sound like?

_____

What would the doorbell store sound like on a
typical day?

_____

What sound would you want YOUR doorbell to make?

_____

Sense Exercise—Smell

Look very carefully at the picture below. Study it closely. Then answer the questions on the next page.

Sense Exercise—Smell

Write your answers on the lines below.

How do the Gridirons smell after a game?

_____

What does the locker room smell like? _____

_____

What do the Gridirons' sneakers smell like? _____

_____

What does Godzilla's shampoo smell like? _____

_____

What does Attila (#65) smell like? _____

_____

What is the Hulk (#5) doing? Does he smell better or worse than the others?_____

What two scents does Genghis (#42) smell? _____

_____

Sense Exercise—Taste and Touch

Look very carefully at the picture below. Study it closely. Then answer the questions on the next page.

Sense Exercise—Taste and Touch

Write your answers on the lines below.

How would the cotton candy taste in your mouth?

_____

How were the two chocolates rated? Which one would be easier

to eat? _____

_____

Would you want to eat the lemon drops? Why or why not?

_____

What was wrong with the tangerine taffy? _____

_____

What should rock candy feel like? _____

_____

What would happen if you picked up the peanut brittle in your hands?

_____

Introduction to Setting—Place

Every story has a setting. The **setting** is the **place** where the story happens. Think of a place that you know well. It could be your room, your kitchen, your backyard, your classroom, or an imaginary place.

Brainstorm some words and ideas about that place. Think about what you see, hear, smell, taste, or feel in that place.

Brainstorm your ideas for a setting below:

Place: _____

_____

_____

_____

_____

_____

_____

_____

_____

_____

Setting—Place

Look at your ideas from the previous page about a setting that interests you and write a paragraph about it. Then draw a picture about your setting in the box below. Remember to include the five senses in your writing.

_____

_____

_____

_____

_____

_____

Name _____   Date _____

The setting is the place where the story happens. But the **setting** is also the **time** in which the story happens. Your reader needs to know when the story is happening. Does your story take place at night? On a sunny day? During winter?

Time can be:

time of day   a holiday   a season of the year

a time in history   a time in the future

The setting also tells the reader **when** the story is happening. Read the following story. Then answer the questions below.

The Cotton Ball Factory!

The cotton ball factory was hot in the summertime, but that didn't stop 300 people from applying for a job as an Official Cotton Ball Tester! It's the best job in the world! To do the job, you had to go to work at midnight, and then sleep on a cotton ball bed made of 1,000,000 cotton balls! In the morning, you had to report how well you slept and whether the cotton balls were soft enough. Sounds like a dream job!

When did this story take place? _____

What time(s) did the story take place? _____

Endings

Finish the story below.

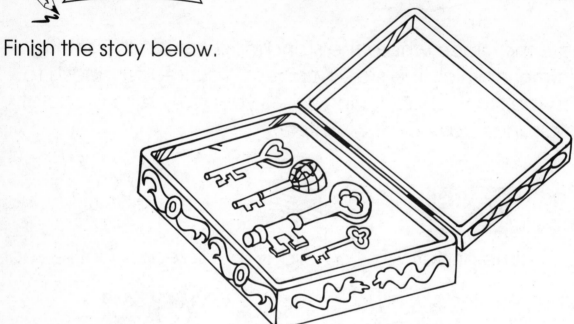

The Four Golden Keys

In a secret room, in the darkest attic, lay buried a hidden box of keys. This was no ordinary box. It was the most beautiful box ever made of exotic woods from ancient forests.

The inside was lined with the plushest red velvet, and on it lay four golden keys. One was very delicate and tiny. The next was large, heavy, and had an ornate handle. The third had a golden orb on top of it. The last one was etched with a heart…

_____

_____

_____

_____

_____

Beginnings and Middles

This story has an ending, but it doesn't have a beginning or middle! Read the ending, and then write a beginning and middle for it. After you are finished, read your story aloud.

The Musical Chair

_____

_____

_____

_____

_____

"We are so sorry! We forgot to tell you about our musical chair before you sat down! It must really like you, because it doesn't sing and dance for everybody, you know!"

The End

0-7682-2784-4 *Gifted & Talented Reading, Writing, and Math*

Brainstorming

Circle one of the idea topics below. Then write down words about that idea.

Idea List

The cookie jar that never became empty!

The night you met the homework fairy!

The girl who loved her new sneakers so much she wore them to bed!

If you were queen or king for the day…

_____

_____

_____

_____

_____

_____

_____

_____

Name _____ Date _____

Narrowing Your Idea

Look at your idea list on the previous page. Use your list to help you write a story about the topic you chose.

_____

_____

_____

_____

_____

_____

_____

_____

_____

_____

_____

_____

0-7682-2784-4 *Gifted & Talented Reading, Writing, and Math*

Story Beginnings

The next story has a middle and an ending, but it doesn't have a beginning! Write a beginning for this story.

The Dancing Piano

_____

_____

_____

_____

There it was again—the sound of four heavy boards stomping and scraping to music! I ran down the stairs to the living room, and sure enough, the piano was doing a jig! "Please, Piano, we know this is your favorite song, but could you please not dance to it at midnight? We have to get some sleep!" I said.

The piano finished its twirl and stopped to rest. I stroked its cover and said, "Piano, we love your music and know how much you love to dance. But please don't play after 10 p.m. so we can sleep, okay?" It played one note in response. From that night on, the piano danced and played until 9:59 p.m., but at the stroke of ten, all became quiet.

The End

70

Name _____   Date _____

Story Middles

This story has a beginning and an ending, but it is missing its middle! Use your imagination and what you read in the story to write a middle. Don't forget to read it aloud after you're finished.

The Clock That Would Tick But Would Not Tock

Oh, it was sad, sad indeed! Ever since we moved Grandma's old clock, something was wrong, something was very wrong. In fact, something was missing! We didn't know if the clock had become damaged during the move, or if it was simply unhappy because we moved it. One thing was certain—the clock would tick, but it would not tock. Sure it would tick, tick, tick, like it was sick, sick, sick, but it simply would not tock!

tick, tick, tick

Can you get Grandma's clock to tock again?

_____

_____

_____

_____

Oh, wow! I forgot what a beautiful sound Grandma's clock makes—a real tick–tock!

The End

71

0-7682-2784-4 *Gifted & Talented Reading, Writing, and Math*

Story Endings

The next few stories have beginnings and middles, but no endings!
Write an ending for each one.

The Leopard and the Zebra

Something very strange happened one night in Africa, on the
Serengeti Plains, to be exact. That night, there was a terrible storm,
a storm that had never been seen by the animals of the Serengeti.
Lightning ripped through the sky, and thunder shook the land beneath
them. On that very night, a leopard and a zebra were born. But
something odd happened: the zebra was born with spots, and the
leopard was born with black and white stripes!

"I'll never be a real zebra! Everybody will
call me 'Spot'!" cried the baby zebra.

"I'll never be a real leopard! Everyone will
call me 'Stripes'!" sighed the baby leopard.

For five years, the zebra wished for stripes, and the leopard wished
for spots. Then one night, a flash of lightning tore through the Serengeti
sky once more....

_____

_____

_____

_____

What If?

Choose your favorite story idea below and brainstorm your ideas on the lines to get ready to write your own story!

What if you found a string hanging from the sky? What is it attached to? If you pulled it, and kept pulling it, and kept pulling it, would it be attached to the moon? To a building? To the other side of the world?

What if you could design any park in the world? What would it have in it? Roller coasters? Jungle forests? Water rides? Twenty Ferris wheels?

What if you found a crystal that let you see into the future? What would you see? What would you do with your crystal? Would you keep it? Give it to the President? Give it to a museum? Keep it a secret?

What if you found a trap door under your bed? Would you open it? Where would it go? Would you tell anybody?

_____

_____

_____

_____

_____

_____

_____

Bringing It All Together

Use your ideas from the previous page to write your own story. Remember, a great story has an exciting beginning, middle, and ending. Good luck!

_____ (title)

By _____

_____

_____

_____

_____

_____

_____

_____

_____

_____

_____

Name _____   Date _____

Making It Better—Describing Words

Remember your adjectives! **Adjectives** are **describing words** that tell us more about something. They make our writing more interesting.

Adjectives tell:

What Kind: red balloon   large hand   ugly shoes

How Many: twenty-five bags   a couple of apples   lots of toys

Which One: those frogs   that table   this bowl

Look at each picture and write a word that describes it.

 _____   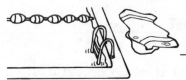 _____

 _____    _____

 _____    _____

0-7682-2784-4 *Gifted & Talented Reading, Writing, and Math*

Making It Better—Describing Words

Remember your adjectives! Descriptive words and details make writing more exciting and offer additional information to the reader.

Beginning (boring!) sentence: The necklace was stolen.

Now let's add some divinely descriptive words!

Adjectives tell:

What Kind: The **sparkling emerald** and **shiny gold** necklace was stolen.

How Many: There is only **one** necklace like this in the world.

Which One: **This** necklace belongs to the Queen of Greece and is worth half-a-billion dollars!

Change the beginning sentences by adding **descriptive words** and **details** to make them more exciting.

1. The ring was lost. _____

2. The tree was in the backyard.

_____

3. The house was painted.

_____

4. Write your own:

_____

Proofreading—Punctuation

Now that you've added exciting descriptive words to your story, it is time for a little proofreading! **Proofreading** helps you fix mistakes in **spelling, punctuation,** and **capitalization**.

First, you must meet Professor Proofhead!

Professor Proofhead would like to show you some exciting proofreading marks.

◯   misspelling   !   add an exclamation mark

≡   make a capital letter   /   change to a lowercase letter

⊙   add a period   ℓ   delete, take out

?   add a question mark   ¶   new paragraph

It is time to practice proofreading. Proofread the following sentences using the marks above.

I wuz Happy two go too my new school

Why r u afraid to sleep inn the dark

We one the grand priz of 1,000,000 pieces of chocolate

I never want want to git in Trubble for being unkind

0-7682-2784-4 *Gifted & Talented Reading, Writing, and Math*

Proofreading—Punctuation

I told mi teacher, Mrs. Dorfman, that that I did knot due mi homework

How many teeth are in your mouth

Proofread the paragraph below.

Another namee name for australia is "The Land Down Under" because it lies entirely in the southern hemisphere Australia is vary unique because it is a continent and all so a countre. The british government helped seddle this vast, beautiful land bye bringing british prisoners their inn 1788. The government had many overcrowded jails and had to come up with a solution They decided decide to send they're prisoners two australia to server there sentences Soon Australiaa attracted other settlers because of it warm, dry climatt and great beauty today it is one of the most beautiful countries on earth, and attracts many tourists who want too visit, "The land Down Under."

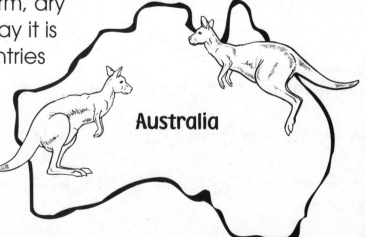

Australia

Final Draft—With Illustration!

Is your story better now that you've added descriptive words? Adjectives help your reader enjoy your story more. Remember, using correct punctuation and spelling makes your story easier to read.

Go ahead and write the final draft of your story (see page 74), and don't forget to include an illustration! After you are finished, read your story aloud.

_____

_____

_____

_____

_____

_____

_____

_____

_____

_____

Name _____   Date _____

Final Draft—With Illustration!

_____

_____

_____

_____

_____

_____

_____

     0-7682-2784-4 *Gifted & Talented Reading, Writing, and Math*

Name _____   Date _____

Three Things You Like About Your Story!

On the lines below, write three things you like best about your story.
Ask yourself: Is my story original? Is it creative? Is it funny? Is it scary?
Is my story filled with mistakes, or is it easy to read?

Favorite thing about my story:

_____

_____

_____

Second favorite thing about my story:

_____

_____

_____

Third favorite thing about my story:

_____

_____

_____

0-7682-2784-4 *Gifted & Talented Reading,*
Writing, and Math

About the Author

Many times in books there is an "About the Author" page that gives readers a little information about the person who wrote the story. It may say where the author was born, where the author went to school (or goes to school!), where the author lives and with whom, and what the author likes to do in his or her free time. Often, a picture of the author is included so readers can see what the author looks like, too!

Use the lines below to write your own "About the Author" page. Attach a picture in the space provided.

_____

_____

_____

_____

_____

_____

_____

_____

_____

Write a Friendly Letter

Friendly letters are fun to write. It's nice to send letters to friends and relatives. It's also nice to receive letters, too! There are rules for writing certain types of letters. Every type of letter is made up of these parts.

> The letter begins with a **greeting**, usually *Dear*, and the name of the person. Always put a comma after the person's name.

> The **date** must go at the top, right-hand side of the letter.

October 2, 2003

Dear Jamie,

    I can't wait to tell you about a story I wrote. It is really exciting, funny, and interesting! It is about a friendly shark that wants to fly! A yellow balloon attached to its belly helps him fly. I hope you like reading my story!

Sincerely,

Conner

> The letter ends with a **closing**. You can write *Sincerely*, or *Yours truly*, *Fondly*, or *Love*. The first word in the closing is always capitalized. Always put a comma after the closing.

> The main part of a letter is called the **body**.

> The writer signs his or her name at the bottom. This is called the **signature**.

Write a Friendly Letter Describing Your Story

Look back at a story you wrote. Write a letter to a friend or relative telling him or her about your story. Some parts of the letter are filled in to help you get started.

_____
(date)

Dear_____,
    (greeting)

_____

_____

_____

_____

_____

_____

(body)

                    Sincerely,
                    (closing)

                  _____
                  (signature)

Survey Says!

Pick at least 10 people (family or friends) for a survey.

Find out how many people:

_____ watch no TV   _____ watch 1-2 hours per day

_____ watch 3-4 hours per day   _____ watch more than 4 hours
                                           per day

Record the ages of the people in each group above.

_____ under 10 years old   _____ 10-15 years old

_____ 16-20 years old   _____ over 20 years old

Record the information in the chart below.

	0 hours	1-2 hours	3-4 hours	over 4 hours
under 10 years old				
10-15				
16-20				
over 20				

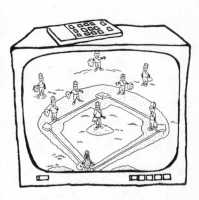

Take a good look at your chart. Can you draw any conclusions about which age group is most likely to watch 2 to 3 hours of TV per day? Explain your answer.

_____

_____

Name _____ Date _____

Day After Day

A year is 365 days long. A week is 7 days. Months can have 28, 29, 30, or 31 days. A fortnight is 14 days. A decade is either 3,652 or 3,653 days.

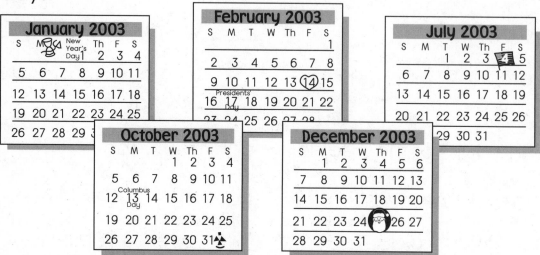

January 2003

S	M	T	W	Th	F	S
	New Year's Day 1	2	3	4		
5	6	7	8	9	10	11
12	13	14	15	16	17	18
19	20	21	22	23	24	25
26	27	28	29			

February 2003

S	M	T	W	Th	F	S
						1
2	3	4	5	6	7	8
9	10	11	12	13	14	15
16	Presidents' Day 17	18	19	20	21	22
23	24	25	26	27	28	

July 2003

S	M	T	W	Th	F	S
		1	2	3	4	5
6	7	8	9	10	11	12
13	14	15	16	17	18	19
20	21	22	23	24	25	26
27	28	29	30	31		

October 2003

S	M	T	W	Th	F	S
			1	2	3	4
5	6	7	8	9	10	11
12	Columbus Day 13	14	15	16	17	18
19	20	21	22	23	24	25
26	27	28	29	30	31	

December 2003

S	M	T	W	Th	F	S
	1	2	3	4	5	6
7	8	9	10	11	12	13
14	15	16	17	18	19	20
21	22	23	24	25	26	27
28	29	30	31			

Arrange the numbers above in order from smallest to largest.

_____

_____

_____

_____

_____

_____

_____

0-7682-2784-4 *Gifted & Talented Reading, Writing, and Math*

Round Up (and Down)!

A rancher has 73 cows. Would it be more accurate to say he has "about 70 cows" or that he has "about 80 cows"?

Circle your answer: about 70   about 80

Another rancher has 278 sheep. Would it be more accurate to say he has "about 200 sheep" or that he has "about 300 sheep"? Round to the nearest hundred.

Circle your answer: about 200   about 300

0-7682-2784-4 *Gifted & Talented Reading, Writing, and Math*

Name _____ Date _____

Round and Round!

A mile is 5,280 feet. Round to the nearest thousand.

Circle your answer: 4,000   5,000   6,000

A dancer spins around twice.
Each spin is 360 degrees. To the
nearest hundred, how many
degrees did the dancer spin?

Circle your answer:

600   700   800

0-7682-2784-4 *Gifted & Talented Reading,*
Writing, and Math

Mental Math!

Add the following numbers in your head:

1. 199 + 36 = _____

2. 200 + 147 = _____

3. 250 + 75 = _____

$$142 + 71 = ?$$

4. 375 + 126 = _____

Subtract the following numbers in your head:

5. 200 − 10 = _____

6. 300 − 23 = _____

7. 400 − 101 = _____

$$200 - 98 = ?$$

8. 250 − 151 = _____

Compute:

9. 1 + 2 + 3 + 4 + 5 + 6 + 7 + 8 + 9 + 10 = _____

10. 10 + 20 + 30 + 40 + 50 + 60 + 70 + 80 + 90 + 100 = _____

11. 10 − 9 + 8 − 7 + 6 − 5 + 4 − 3 + 2 − 1 = _____

12. 100 − 90 + 80 − 70 + 60 − 50 + 40 − 30 + 20 − 10 = _____

Sums and Differences

Compute. Show your work.

1. $1 + 23 + 456 + 7,890$ = _____

2. $2,000 - 456$ = _____

3. $1 + 100 + 10 + 1,000 + 10,000$ = _____

4. $3,000,000 - 234,567$ = _____

5. $2,345 - 400 + 399$ = _____

6. $369 + 725 - 368$ = _____

Close Enough Is Still Good Enough!

Estimate the answers below to the nearest ten. Do **not** work out the exact answer.

1. 341 + 52 = _____

2. 341 – 52 = _____

3. 667 + 125 = _____

4. 667 – 125 = _____

5. 511 + 495 = _____

6. 511 – 495 = _____

7. 407 + 291 = _____

8. 407 – 291 = _____

9. 234 + 379 + 99 + 305 = _____

10. 2,989 + 34 + 5,102 + 899 = _____

11. 10,000 – 2,001 – 4,981 – 999 – 1,005 = _____

 Mental Math!

Multiply the following numbers in your head:

1. 4 x 125 = _____

2. 5 x 64 = _____

3. 10 x 37 = _____

4. 100 x 432 = _____

Divide the following numbers in your head:

5. 200 ÷ 50 = _____   6. 300 ÷ 2 = _____

7. 400 ÷ 4 = _____   8. 150 ÷ 25 = _____

Compute. Show your work.

9. 12,345,679 x 8 = _____

10. 6,420,864 ÷ 2 = _____

0-7682-2784-4 *Gifted & Talented Reading Writing, and Math*

Name _____   Date _____

More Mental Math!

Multiply the following numbers in your head:

1. 8 x 225 = _____

2. 10 x 420 = _____

3. 50 x 60 = _____

4. 100 x 360 = _____

Divide the following numbers in your head:

5. 1,000 ÷ 50 = _____   **6.** 300 ÷ 20 = _____

7. 4,000 ÷ 40 = _____   **8.** 2,500 ÷ 250 = _____

Compute. Show your work.

9. 12,345,679 x 27 = _____

10. 18,200 ÷ 14 = _____

0-7682-2784-4 *Gifted & Talented Reading, Writing, and Math*

Give Them an Inch

There are 12 inches in a foot and 5,280 feet in a mile. Use a calculator to figure out how many half-inches there are in a mile.

1 mile
5,280 feet
? inches

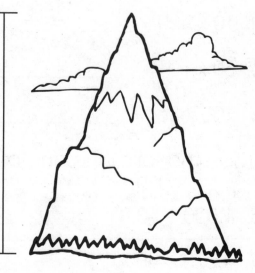

Use your calculator to do the following problems:

1. 12,345,679 x 9 = _____

2. 12,345,679 x 18 = _____

3. 12,345,679 x 27 = _____

4. 12,345,679 x 36 = _____

Do you see the pattern? Without using your calculator, what is:

5. 12,345,679 x 72 = _____

6. 12,345,679 x ____ = 555,555,555

0-7682-2784-4 *Gifted & Talented Reading,*
Writing, and Math

Name _____   Date _____

Darling Decimals!

Oh, those darling decimals! They can be tricky! When working with decimals, it often is helpful to think about what we know about money.

10.25

For example, 7 + 1.25 can be thought of as $7.00 + $1.25, and 6.7 - 2.65 can be thought of as $6.70 - $2.65.

Calculate. Show your work.

1. 3 + 4.56 = _____

2. 5.67 + 3.9 = _____

3. 12.3 + 3.12 = _____

4. 15.67 + 123 = _____

5. 8 – 2.25 = _____

6. 12.75 – 3.2 = _____

7. 7 – 4.56 = _____

8. 12.3 – 4 = _____

Name _____   Date _____

The Next Number, Please!

Write the next three numbers in each of the following number patterns:

1. 1, 2, 4, 7, 11, _____, _____, _____

2. 1, 11, 10, 20, 19, _____, _____, _____

3. 1, 2, 4, 8, 16, _____, _____, _____

4. 1, 4, 9, 16, 25, _____, _____, _____

5. 0, 1, 1, 2, 3, 5, 8, 13, _____, _____, _____

6. 32, 16, 8, 4, 2, _____, _____, _____

Picture This!

Answer each question. Then draw a figure that completes each group.

1. What is the same about each figure? _____

 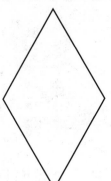 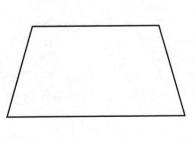

2. What is the same about each figure? _____

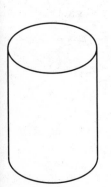 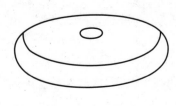

3. What is the same about each figure? _____

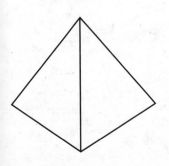 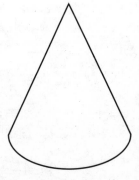 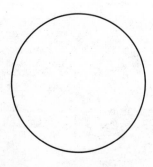

Help Harpo, Henrietta, and Hank!

Help Harpo figure out the total value of the coins in his piggy bank.

1. Find the total value of the coins in the picture.

Total = $ _____._____

Help Henrietta figure out the total value of the coins in her piggy bank.

2. Find the total value of the coins in the picture.

Total = $ _____._____

Help Hank figure out the total value of the coins and bills in his shoe box.

3. Find the total value of the bills and coins in the picture.

Total = $ _____._____

0-7682-2784-4 *Gifted & Talented Reading,*
Writing, and Math

Name _____   Date _____

Missing Money!

Harpo's sister, Hanna, decided to count the money in her change purse and her piggy bank.

Find the total value of the bills and coins shown in the picture.

Total = $ _____._____

Hanna has a problem. The last time she counted the money from her piggy bank, she put a note on it saying, "This bank contains only dimes and quarters. It contains a total of $4.50. There are 10 quarters and _____ dimes."

The problem is that the number of dimes got smudged out. Without actually counting the coins, how can Hanna figure out how many dimes are in the bank?

This bank contains only dimes and quarters. It contains a total of $4.50. There are 10 quarters and 🪙 dimes.

Number of dimes = _____

Explain how you found your answer.

_____

_____

0-7682-2784-4 *Gifted & Talented Reading, Writing, and Math*

Name _____   Date _____

After every five tickets are sold, the ticket seller at the carnival records the amount of money he has taken in so far. Look at his chart below:

Tickets	5	10	15	20	25	30	35	40	45	50
Total	$12.50	$25.00	$37.50							

After 25 tickets are sold, how much money will be recorded in the chart?

1. Total = $ _____._____

After 40 tickets are sold, how much money will be recorded in the chart?

2. Total = $ _____._____

After 50 tickets are sold, how much money will be recorded in the chart?

3. Total = $ _____._____

Red, White, and Blue!

Half of the marbles in a bag are red.
A quarter of the marbles are white.
The rest are blue.

1. What fractional part of the marbles
   is blue? _____

  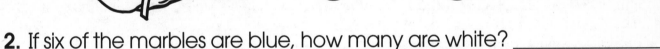

2. If six of the marbles are blue, how many are white? _____

3. How many total marbles are there in the bag? _____

4. Twelve blue marbles are
   added to the bag. What
   fractional part of the
   marbles is now blue?

   _____

5. What fractional part of
   the marbles is now white?

   _____

How Much?

Half-of-a-quarter of a piece of cheese weighs 6 ounces. How much does the whole piece weigh?

1. Total weight = _____ ounces = _____ pounds

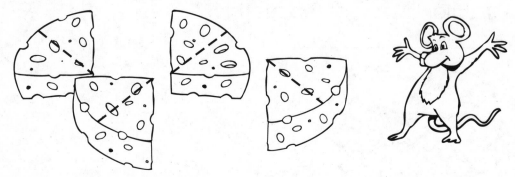

A sandbox is half full. When 200 pounds of sand are added, the box contains 750 pounds of sand. How much sand will the sandbox hold?

2. The sandbox will hold _____ pounds of sand.

3. How much of the football game is left half way through the second quarter? _____

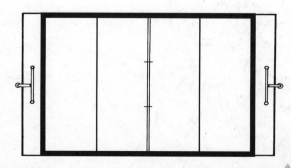

Straight From the Horse's Mouth!

A furlong is a unit of measure used mostly in horse racing. A furlong is one-eighth ($\frac{1}{8}$) of a mile.

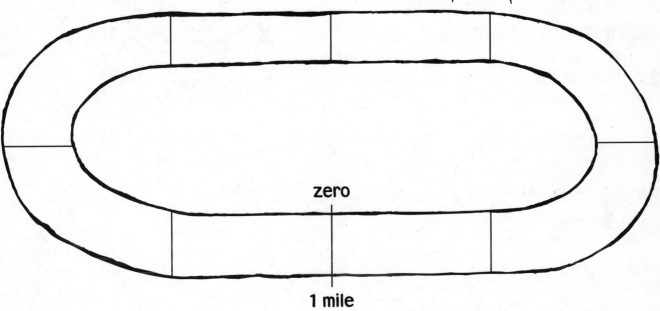

zero

1 mile

1. What fractional part of a mile is 4 furlongs? _____

2. What fractional part of a mile is 6 furlongs? _____

3. What fractional part of a mile is $7\frac{1}{2}$ furlongs? _____

4. How many furlongs are in $\frac{1}{4}$ of a mile? _____

5. How many furlongs are in $1\frac{3}{16}$ of a mile? _____

1. Three times a certain number, minus 1, equals 32. Find the number.

$$3 \times \underline{\qquad} - 1 = 32$$

The number of bacteria in a jar doubles every day. After 20 days, the jar is full. When was the jar half full?

2. The jar was half full on the
   _____ day.

Who is the better free-throw shooter, Freddie or Jamie?

Freddie made 17 out of 24 free throws.

Jamie made 8 out of 12 free throws.

3. _____ is the better shooter.

Explain your answer.

_____

_____

_____

Name _____   Date _____

City to City

The distance from City 1 to City 2 is 100 miles. The distance from City 2 to City 3 is 25 miles.

City 1   City 2

1. What is the **maximum** distance possible between City 1 and City 3?

Maximum distance = _____ miles

2. What is the **minimum** distance possible between City 1 and City 3?

Minimum distance = _____ miles

3. On the map, draw a picture of all the possible locations of City 3.

City 1   City 2

0-7682-2784-4 *Gifted & Talented Reading, Writing, and Math*

Name _____   Date _____

 Captain Chris!

Captain Chris is organizing his charts. Help him complete the charts below.

1. Complete the following chart:

1 + 2 + 3 + . . .	+ 9 + 10 = 55
1 + 2 + 3 + . . .	+ 99 + 100 = 5,050
1 + 2 + 3 + . . .	+ 999 + 1,000 = 500,500
1 + 2 + 3 + . . .	+ 9,999 + 10,000 = _____
1 + 2 + 3 + . . .	+ 1,000,000 = _____
1 + 2 + 3 + . . .	+ 1_____ = 5,000,050,000

2. Complete the following chart:

11 x 11 =	121
111 x 111 =	12,321
1,111 x 1,111 =	1,234,321
11,111 x 11,111 =	_____
1,111,111 x 1,111,111 =	_____
_____ x _____	= 12,345,654,321

Wacky Widgets!

Ten widgets cost $2.50. (One widget costs a quarter.)

25¢

1. How much do nine widgets cost? _____

   Explain your answer. _____

   _____

2. How much do 12 widgets cost? _____

   Explain your answer. _____

   _____

3. How much do 20 widgets cost? _____

   Explain your answer. _____

   _____

4. How much do 5 widgets cost? _____

   Explain your answer. _____

   _____

5. How much do 30 widgets cost? _____

   Explain your answer. _____

Some Like It Hot!

Water freezes at 32 degrees Fahrenheit and boils at 212 degrees. Water freezes at 0 degrees Celsius and boils at 100 degrees.

How many degrees is it from freezing to boiling on the Fahrenheit scale? _____

How many degrees is it from freezing to boiling on the Celsius scale? _____

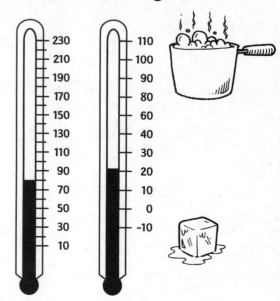

The water in each pan on the stove is exactly the same temperature. The heat in the pan on the left went up 1 degree Fahrenheit. The heat in the pan on the right went up 1 degree Celsius.

Which pan now has the hotter water?

   Circle one: left pan   right pan

Explain your answer. _____

_____

_____

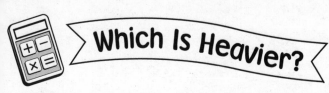

Which Is Heavier?

One kilogram is about 2.2 pounds.

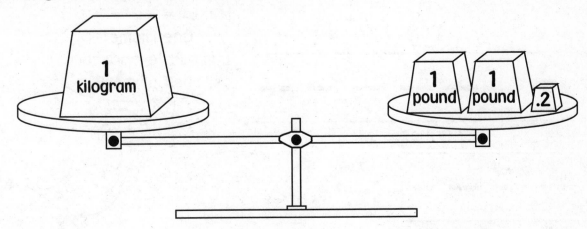

1. About how many pounds does a 50-kilogram sack of coffee beans weigh? _____

2. Does a fish that weighs 10 pounds weigh more or less than 5 kilograms?

   _____

3. Is a pound more or less than half of a kilogram?

   Circle one: more   less

Explain your answer. _____

_____

_____

0-7682-2784-4 *Gifted & Talented Reading, Writing, and Math*

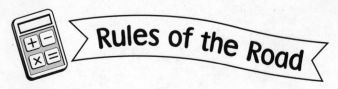

Rules of the Road

One kilometer is a little more than half of a mile. (1 km = 0.6 miles)

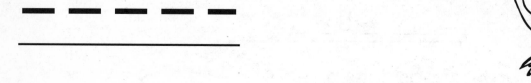

One kilometer is a little more than half of a mile.

Is 10 kilometers more or less than 5 miles? _____

Two cars start driving from City A to City B. The first car travels at a steady rate of 40 kilometers per hour. The second car travels at a steady rate of 40 miles per hour. Which car gets to City B first?

Circle one: Car 1   Car 2

Is a mile more or less than two kilometers?

Circle one: more   less

Explain your answer. _____

_____

_____

0-7682-2784-4 *Gifted & Talented Reading, Writing, and Math*

Inch by Inch

One inch is exactly 2.54 centimeters.

One inch is exactly 2.54 centimeters.

1 inch

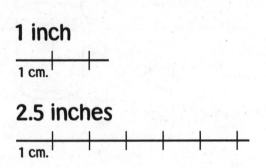

2.5 inches

1. Is 10 centimeters more or less than five inches? _____

2. A yard is 36 inches. About how many centimeters is this?

   Circle one: 20   40   60   80   90   100

3. Is a centimeter more or less than half of an inch?

   Circle one: more   less

Explain your answer. _____

_____

_____

Name _____   Date _____

How Much?

One liter is a little more than one quart.

Four quarts make a gallon.

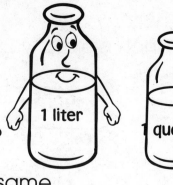

1. Which is bigger: two liters or half-a-gallon?

Circle one: two liters   half-a-gallon   same

Two cups make a pint.

Two pints make a quart.

2. About how many pints are there in a liter? Remember, a liter is a little more than a quart.

Circle one: 1 to 2   2 to 3   3 to 4   4 to 5

Explain your answer. _____

_____

_____

Name _____   Date _____

Ranch Hands!

A rancher has 60 yards of fencing to make a corral for some of his horses.

1. If he makes the corral in a square, how long will each side be? _____

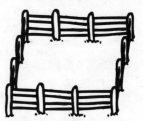

2. If the corral is in the shape of a rectangle, and the length is 20 yards, how long is the width? _____

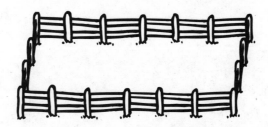

3. The rancher finally decides to put the corral next to his barn. That way he has to fence in only three sides of it. The long side, which is parallel to the barn, will be 40 yards. How long will each of the other sides be? _____

0-7682-2784-4 *Gifted & Talented Reading, Writing, and Math*

How Far Around?

1. Find the perimeter of a triangle whose sides are 2 inches, $3\frac{1}{2}$ inches, and $4\frac{3}{4}$ inches.

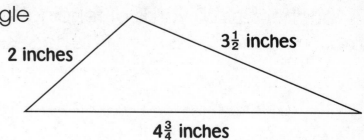

2 inches

$3\frac{1}{2}$ inches

$4\frac{3}{4}$ inches

_____

2. Find the perimeter of a hexagon whose sides are all $2\frac{1}{2}$ inches.

$2\frac{1}{2}$ inches

_____

3. Find the length of the side of a square whose perimeter is 30 meters.

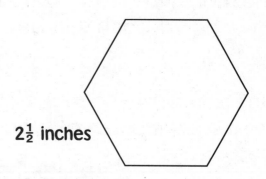

perimeter = 30 meters

_____

4. Find the length of the side of an octagon whose perimeter is 26 feet.

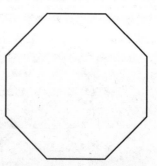

perimeter = 26 feet

_____

0-7682-2784-4 *Gifted & Talented Reading, Writing, and Math*

Name _____   Date _____

1. Find the area of a square whose sides are each 5 feet.

5 feet

2. The area of a square is 36 square inches. Find the perimeter of the square.

area = 36 sq. in.

3. Which has the greater area: a square whose sides are each 10 inches or a circle whose diameter is 10 inches?

Circle one: the square   the circle

 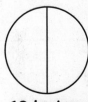

10 inches   **10 inches**

The length of the side of a square is doubled.

4. What is the relationship between the perimeters of the two squares?

Circle one: the perimeters are the same
                the new perimeter is twice of the old
                the new perimeter is half of the old
                the new perimeter is four times the old

5. What is the relationship between the areas of the two squares?

Circle one: the areas are the same
                the new square is twice as big
                the new square is half as a big
                the new square is four times as big

0-7682-2784-4 *Gifted & Talented Reading, Writing, and Math*

Coin Toss!

Three coins are tossed. Make a list of all the possible combinations of heads and tails that can occur. (Hint: There are **8 ways** that 3 coins can come up.)

_____   _____

_____   _____

_____   _____

This time, 4 coins are tossed. Make a list of all the possible combinations of heads and tails that can occur. (Hint: There are **16 ways** that 3 coins can come up.)

_____   _____

_____   _____

_____   _____

_____   _____

0-7682-2784-4 *Gifted & Talented Reading, Writing, and Math*

Name _____   Date _____

Nick has a regular deck of 52 playing cards.

He picks one card from the deck. How many of the cards are "winners" if he wants the card to be a red card?

_____

Nick puts the card he picked back in the deck and picks another card. How many of the cards are "winners" if he wants the card to be a face card (a jack, queen, or king)?

_____

Again he puts the card he picked back in the deck and picks another card. How many of the cards are "winners" if he wants the card to be a prime number (a 2, 3, 5, or 7)?

_____

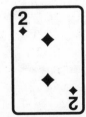   

0-7682-2784-4 *Gifted & Talented Reading, Writing, and Math*

Fair Share!

Martha and George take turns baby-sitting. Martha works for 4 hours and George works for 2 hours. They are paid $24.00. How should they share the money? _____

4 hours = ??? dollars

2 hours = ??? dollars

One ton of sand is to be put into 50–pound bags. Each bag will sell for $5.00. How much is the sand worth? _____

0-7682-2784-4 *Gifted & Talented Reading, Writing, and Math*

Name _____   Date _____

How Much?

A family wants to travel 1,000 miles in four days by car. On the first day, they traveled 275 miles. On the second day, they covered 245 miles. How many miles must they average on **each** of the next two days?

_____

day 1—275 miles
day 2—245 miles
day 3—
day 4—

A girl put $25.00 in the bank. Each week for 12 weeks she deposited $5.50 more. Then she took out $12.75. How much was left in the account? _____

BANK

An aquarium is three-fourths full of water. Half of the water leaks out. How full is the aquarium now? _____

0-7682-2784-4 *Gifted & Talented Reading, Writing, and Math*

On Average

7 is soooo average!

Find the average of 4, 5, 7, and 12.

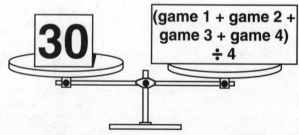

_____

Find the average of 10, 15, and 65. _____

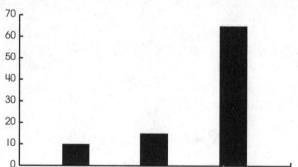

The average of three numbers is 15. Two of the numbers are 15 and 10. Find the third number.

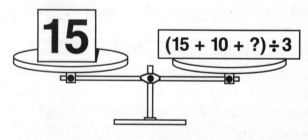

_____

Michael had an average of 30 points per game for four games. How many total points did he score?

_____

Easy as Pie!

Shade-in ½ of the first circle.

Shade-in ²⁄₄ of the first circle.
What is another name for this amount? _____

Shade-in ¾ of the first circle.

Shade-in ⁴⁄₄ of the first circle.

Shade-in ⁷⁄₄.

Shade-in ⁵⁄₄.

Shade-in ⁸⁄₄.

Shade-in ⁶⁄₄.

Shade-in ¹¹⁄₄.

121

0-7682-2784-4 *Gifted & Talented Reading, Writing, and Math*

Excellent Eggs!

A dozen eggs cost $1.50.

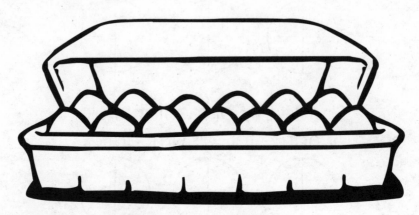

1. How much do three dozen eggs cost? _____

2. How much do 60 eggs cost? _____

3. How much does a half dozen eggs cost? _____

4. How much does one egg cost? _____

5. How much does a gross (12 dozen) of eggs cost? _____

6. How much do $2\frac{1}{2}$ dozen eggs cost? _____

7. How many eggs can you buy for $6.00? _____

8. How many eggs can you buy for $9.00? _____

The King and the Doctor

One day, a king summoned the royal doctor. The king's son was very sick. "Save my son's life," commanded the king, "and I will give you any amount of money you ask."

After several days, the king's son was restored to health by the doctor. "Thank you, Doctor," said the king. "What do you request as payment?"

"A checkerboard has 8 rows and 8 columns, 64 squares in all. Place I penny on the first square, 2 pennies on the second square, 4 pennies on third square, 8 pennies on the fourth square, and keep doubling, until you reach the 64th square. I will take the amount on the 64th square. This will be payment enough," said the doctor.

The king offered the doctor ten million dollars instead. Should the doctor accept the king's offer? Why or why not?

_____

_____

_____

How much money will be on the 64th square? _____

0-7682-2784-4 *Gifted & Talented Reading, Writing, and Math*

Stars and Stripes Forever!

Each American flag has 50 stars and 13 stripes.

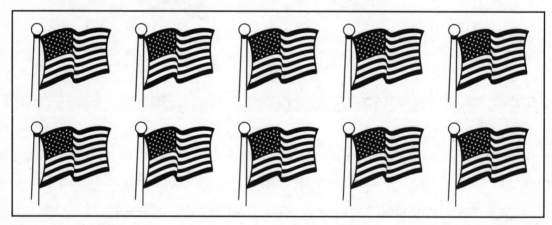

1. How many **stars** are there in the picture? _____

2. How many **stripes**? _____

3. How many **more** flags are needed to have exactly 750 stars?

_____

4. How many stripes are there on 25 flags? _____

5. How many flags can be made out of 2,000 stars? _____

At a Theater Near You!

There is a movie theater with 10 rows of seats. Each row has 15 seats. Tickets to the movie theater cost $6.00 each.

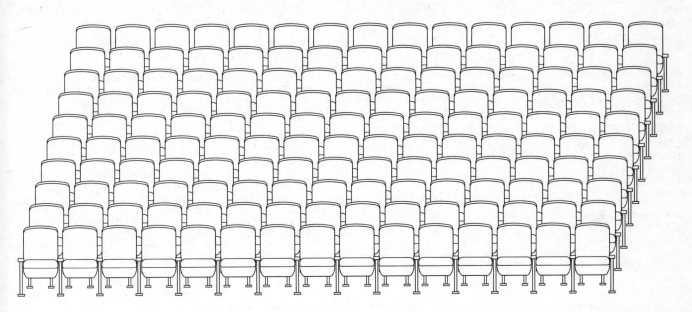

1. How many total seats are there in the theater? _____

2. How much money does the theater take in if there is a full house?

_____

3. How much money does the theater take in if all but the last two rows are filled?

_____

4. How much money does the theater take in if all but the last $2\frac{1}{3}$ rows are filled?

_____

0-7682-2784-4 *Gifted & Talented Reading, Writing, and Math*

Answer Key

Circle a Synonym!   Page 5
1. wealthy, rich
2. plain, easy
3. fake, processed
4. brave, daring
5. attire, same
6. help, assist

Synonym Stars!   Page 6
Speeches will vary.

Antonyms are Opposites!   Page 7
1. intelligent, stupid
2. confident, unsure
3. defend, attack
4. energetic, lazy

Antonym Puzzle!   Page 8
ACROSS
1. cheap
4. seldom
6. nonfiction
7. rude
DOWN
2. awkward
3. more
4. synonym
5. gentle

Different Meanings   Page 9
2, 5, 6
4, 1, 7, 3

Check, Please!   Page 10
1. B
2. A
3. A
4. B
5. A

Common Corrections!   Page 11
1. their
2. accept, there
3. their, except
4. angels, angle
5. intend, attend, their

More Common Corrections!   Page 12
1. series
2. loose
3. bear
4. serious
5. lose
6. bare

Claudio's Context Clues!   Page 13
1. grow
2. touch
3. walking
4. fun
5. announced

What Do You Mean?   Page 14
1. fat
2. shouting
3. awful
4. strutting
5. empty

Mind the Mold!   Page 15
3, 2, 1

Figure It Out!   Pages 16–17
1. Melanie tried to remain serious.
2. Joey plans to study every night.
3. The gerbil made the girls very tired.
4. The rain would be severe and heavy.
5. Liza is a successful gardener.
6. Do not worry about the small things.

More About the Recycler!   Page 19
Answers will vary.

Amundsen-Scott Station   Page 21
Answers will vary.

Happy Kwanzaa!   Page 22
1. Kwanzaa takes place December 26 through January 1.
2. On December 31, in the evening, Aisha's relatives come over to celebrate the Kwanzaa feast.

When and Where?   Page 23
1. at night, in the winter
2. San Juan, Puerto Rico
3. last June
4. the beautiful beaches of Costa Rica
5. in November
6. at the Championship Game at Rigby Field

Make a Map!   Page 24
Maps will vary.

Suzette La Fleur!   Pages 26–27
1. informational passage
2. autobiography
3. biography
4. Answers will vary.

Okay, So How Do They Do It?   Page 29
6, 1, 3, X, X, X, 5, 2, X, X, 4, X

Dirt Cake!   Pages 31–32
1. A
2. C
3. A
4. B
5. B
6. C
7. Answers will vary.

Mindy Gets the Main Idea!   Page 33
1. Sammy is unselfish.
2. Jamie is an intelligent businessman.
3. Mr. Waterford enjoys visiting fast-food places.

Flying Penguins   Page 34
C

Highlight Happy!   Page 35
1. Columbus, Ohio; Columbia, South Carolina; Bismarck, North Dakota; Pierre, South Dakota; Springfield, Illinois
2. Answers will vary.

Cause and Effect   Page 36
Effect: Walter was extremely excited to learn more about Picasso's art.

How Did It Happen?   Page 37
1. James set his watch back 6 hours.
2. Trudy's back ached because she had lifted heavy boxes all day long.

Who Invented the Ice-Cream Cone?   Page 39
1. Italo invented the ice-cream cone in 1896.
2. Italo was granted a patent in 1903.
3. The ice-cream vendor ran out of bowls to serve his ice cream.
4. Mr. Hamwi had an idea to solve the ice-cream vendor's problem.
5. The rest is ice-cream history!

Parnel Picks Some Pets!   Page 41
Answers will vary.

500 Apples!   Page 42
Answers will vary.

What Happens Next?   Page 43
Answers will vary.

Naming Words—Nouns   Page 44
Circle: chef, island, coast, Ireland, name, Happy O'Reilly, people, world, Happy, cheeks, eyes, smile, everybody, cottage, fireplace, bread, stew, sickness, summertime, dessert, smile, face, year, Happy O'Reilly

Action Words—Verbs   Page 45
answers, studies, eats, chats, race, yell, read, play
Sentences will vary.

Describing Words— Adjectives   Page 46
1. soft, expensive, thousands
2. hairy, black, ugly
3. scary, hungry, tall, loud
4. delicate, beautiful

Sentences—Complete Thoughts   Page 47
1. fragment
2. sentence
3. sentence
4. fragment
5. fragment
6-9. Sentences will vary.

Types of Sentences   Page 49
1. declarative
2. exclamatory
3. interrogative
4. imperative
5. exclamatory
6. interrogative
7. declarative
8. exclamatory
Sentences will vary.

The Commas Are Coming!   Page 51
1. My three favorite types of foods are spinach, ice cream, and ham.
2. "Did you eat, Jim?" Molly asked sincerely.
3. According to Billy, Molly and Jim were up late last night trying to find apples, cheese, and desserts.
4. Looking back at her younger brother, Molly stuck out her tongue!
5. After she left her aunt, Susan started to cry.

0-7682-2784-4 *Gifted & Talented Reading, Writing, and Math*

Transition Words   Page 52
Circle: First, Next, After, Then, Finally

Using Transition Words   Page 53
Students should use the transition words
First, Next, Then, Finally, Last.

Introducing the Five Senses   Page 54
Answers will vary.

Sense Exercise—Sight   Page 56
1. Astro Burgers and Space Fries
2. filling up their gas tank
3. sunlight
4. brown lunch bags
5. space fries

Sense Exercise—Sound   Page 58
Answers will vary.

Sense Exercise—Smell   Page 60
Answers will vary.

Sense Exercise—Taste and Touch   Page 62
Answers will vary.

Introduction to Setting—Place   Page 63
Answers will vary.

Setting—Place   Page 64
Answers will vary.

Setting—Time   Page 65
in the summertime at midnight, in the morning

Endings   Page 66
Story endings will vary.

Beginnings and Middles   Page 67
Story beginnings and middles will vary.

Brainstorming   Page 68
Answers will vary.

Narrowing Your Idea   Page 69
Stories will vary.

Story Beginnings   Page 70
Story beginnings will vary.

Story Middles   Page 71
Story middles will vary.

Story Endings   Page 72
Story endings will vary.

Bringing It All Together   Pages 73–74
Answers will vary.

Making It Better—Describing Words   Page 75
Answers will vary.

Making It Better—Describing Words   Page 76
Answers will vary.

Proofreading—Punctuation   Page 77
I wuz happy two go too my new school.
Why RU afraid to sleep inn the dark?
We one the grand prize of 1,000,000 pieces of chocolate.
I never want want to git in trubble for being unkind.

Proofreading—Punctuation   Page 78
I told my teacher, Mrs. Dorfman, that I did knot due mi homework.
How many teeth are in your mouth?
Another namee name for australia is "The Land Down Under"
because it lies entirely in the southern hemisphere. Australia is vary
unique because it is a continent and all so a countrie. The british
government helped seddle this vast, beautiful land bye bringing
british prisoners thear inn 1788. The government had many
overcrowded jails and had to come up with a solution. They decided
dede to send they're prisoners two australia to server there.
sentence. Soon Australia attracted
other settlers because of it warm, dry
climat and great beauty. today it is
one of the most beautiful countries
on earth, and attracts many
tourists who want too visit,
"The land Down Under."

Final Draft—With Illustration   Pages 79–80
Stories will vary.

Three Things you Like About Your Story!   Page 81
Answers will vary.

About the Author   Page 82
Answers will vary.

Write a Friendly Letter Describing Your Story   Page 84
Letters will vary.

Survey Says!   Page 85
Answers will vary.

Day After Day   Page 86
7; 14; 28; 29; 30; 31; 365; 3,652; 3,653

Round Up (and Down)!   Page 87
about 70; about 300

Round and Round!   Page 88
5,000; 700

Mental Math!   Page 89
1. 235
2. 347
3. 325
4. 501
5. 190
6. 277
7. 299
8. 99
9. 55
10. 550
11. 5
12. 50

Sums and Differences   Page 90
1. 8,370
2. 1,544
3. 11,111
4. 2,765,433
5. 2,344
6. 726

Close Enough Is Still Good Enough!   Page 91
1. 390
2. 290
3. 800
4. 540
5. 1,010
6. 10
7. 700
8. 120
9. 1,020
10. 9,020
11. 1,010

Mental Math!   Page 92
1. 500
2. 320
3. 370
4. 43,200
5. 4
6. 150
7. 100
8. 6
9. 98,765,432
10. 3,210,432

More Mental Math!   Page 93
1. 1,800
2. 4,200
3. 3,000
4. 36,000
5. 20
6. 15
7. 100
8. 10
9. 333,333,333
10. 1,300

Give Them an Inch   Page 94
126,720 half-inches
1. 111,111,111
2. 222,222,222
3. 333,333,333
4. 444,444,444
5. 888,888,888
6. 45

Darling Decimals!   Page 95
1. 7.56
2. 9.57
3. 15.42
4. 138.67
5. 5.75
6. 9.55
7. 2.44
8. 8.3

The Next Number, Please!   Page 96
1. 16, 22, 29
2. 29, 28, 38
3. 32, 64, 128
4. 36, 49, 64
5. 21, 34, 55
6. $1, \frac{1}{2}, \frac{1}{4}$

Picture This!   Page 97
Figures may vary.
1. They are all flat figures with straight edges. They all have 4 sides.
2. They are all circular, 3-dimensional figures.
3. They are all 3-dimensional figures.

Help Harpo, Henrietta, and Hank!   Page 98
1. $4.19
2. $7.78
3. $18.63

Missing Money!   Page 99
$96.70; 20 dimes
Hannah knows that there are 10 quarters,
which equals $2.50 of the total amount.
That leaves $2.00 worth of dimes, which
equals 20 dimes.

One for the Money! — Page 100
1. $62.50
2. $100.00
3. $125.00

Red, White, and Blue! — Page 101
1. $\frac{1}{4}$
2. 6
3. 24 marbles
4. $\frac{1}{2}$ are now blue
5. $\frac{1}{6}$ are now white

How Much? — Page 102
1. 48 oz. = 3 lb.
2. 1,100 lbs. of sand
3. $\frac{5}{8}$ is left

Straight From the Horse's Mouth! — Page 103
1. $\frac{1}{2}$ mile
2. $\frac{3}{4}$ mile
3. $\frac{15}{16}$ mile
4. 2 furlongs
5. $9\frac{1}{2}$ furlongs

Logic It Out! — Page 104
1. 11
2. 19th
3. Freddie is the better shooter since $\frac{17}{24}$ is greater than $\frac{8}{12}$ ($\frac{16}{24}$).

City to City — Page 105
1. Maximum distance = 125 miles
2. Minimum distance = 75 miles
3. City 3 could be 25 miles to the left of City 2 or 25 miles to the right of City 2. Or, City 3 could also be in any position 25 miles vertically or diagonally from City 2, but this will not give you the minimum and maximum distance.

Captain Chris! — Page 106
1. 50,005,000; 500,000,500,000; 100,000
2. 123,454,321; 1,234,567,654,321; 111,111 x 111,111

Wacky Widgets! — Page 107
1. $2.25; multiply $0.25 by 9
2. $3.00; multiply $0.25 by 12
3. $5.00; multiply $0.25 by 20
4. $1.25; multiply $0.25 by 5
5. $7.50; multiply $0.25 by 30

Some Like It Hot! — Page 108
180 degrees Fahrenheit
100 degrees Celsius
Circle: right pan
The right pan is hotter because one degree Celsius equals 2.12 degrees Fahrenheit. One degree Celsius is greater than one degree Fahrenheit.

Which Is Heavier? — Page 109
1. 110 pounds
2. Less than 5 kilograms.
3. Circle: less
One kilogram is equal to 2.2 pounds. Half of a kilogram is equal to 1.1 pounds. So, one pound is less than half a kilogram.

Rules of the Road — Page 110
More than 5 miles
Circle: car 2
Circle: less; One kilometer is equal to 0.6 mile. Therefore, two kilometers is equal to 1.2 miles. So, one mile is less than 2 kilometers.

Inch by Inch — Page 111
1. less
2. Circle: 90
3. Circle: less; Half of an inch is equal to 1.27 centimeters. Therefore, one centimeter is less than half an inch.

How Much? — Page 112
1. Circle: two liters
2. Circle: 4 to 5; There are four pints in a quart. A liter is a little more than a quart. So, 4 to 5 pints are in one liter.

Ranch Hands! — Page 113
1. 15 yards
2. 10 yards
3. 10 yards each

How Far Around? — Page 114
1. $10\frac{1}{4}$ inches
2. 15 inches
3. $7\frac{1}{2}$ meters
4. $3\frac{1}{4}$ feet

The Plane Facts — Page 115
1. 25 feet
2. 24 inches
3. Circle: square
4. Circle: the new perimeter is twice of the old
5. Circle: the new square is four times as big

Coin Toss! — Page 116
3 coins: HHH, HHT, HTH, THH, HTT, TTH, THT, TTT
4 coins: HHHH, HHHT, HHTH, HTHH, THHH, HHTT, HTHT, HTTH, THTH, TTHH, THHT, HTTT, THTT, TTHT, TTTH, TTTT

52 Cards — Page 117
26 cards; 12 cards; 16 cards

Fair Share! — Page 118
Martha: $16, George: $8
$200

How Much? — Page 119
240 miles; $78.25; $\frac{3}{8}$ full

On Average — Page 120
7; 30; 20; 120 points

Easy as Pie! — Page 121
Shade-in $\frac{1}{2}$ of the first circle.

Shade-in $\frac{2}{4}$ of the first circle.
What is another name for this amount? ___half___

Shade-in $\frac{2}{4}$ of the first circle.

Shade-in $\frac{1}{4}$ of the first circle.   Shade-in $\frac{3}{4}$.

Shade-in $\frac{2}{4}$.   Shade-in $\frac{5}{4}$.

Shade-in $\frac{4}{4}$.   Shade-in $\frac{11}{4}$.

Excellent Eggs! — Page 122
1. $4.50
2. $7.50
3. $0.75
4. about $0.13
5. $18.00
6. $3.75
7. 48 eggs
8. 72 eggs

The King and the Doctor — Page 123
The doctor should not accept the king's offer. After square 23, you're already over the $10 million.
The amount in the 64th square is 9,223,372,036,854,775,808 cents (9 quintillion cents) or $92,233,720,368,547,758.08 (92 quadrillion dollars).

Stars and Stripes Forever! — Page 124
1. 500 stars
2. 130 stripes
3. 5 more flags
4. 325 stripes
5. 40 flags

At a Theater Near You! — Page 125
1. 150 seats
2. $900
3. $720
4. $690

0-7682-2784-4 *Gifted & Talented Reading, Writing, and Math*